Petals of the Unsaid

Poems of Unspoken Emotions, Love, and Life's Silent Truths

Deepa Krishnamurthy

Made with ❤ on the BookLeaf Publishing Platform
www.bookleafpub.in
www.bookleafpub.com

Dedication

To my ride-or-die partner, Shijith—for being my unwavering cheerleader, standing by me with endless support and encouragement. Your belief in me has been my greatest strength, and for that, I am eternally grateful.

Acknowledgements

To you, the reader, who dares to dive into the depths of unspoken emotions—may these poems find a home in the quiet corners of your heart. Thank you for letting my words echo your own unvoiced feelings and shared moments of love, life, and reflection.

To my soul sisters & best friends, who are my chosen family; for having shown me the beauty of vulnerability and having taught me the courage to wear my heart on my sleeve.

To my cherished school teacher and role model, Ms. Odelia, who has always reminded me to embrace my authenticity, and to live freely and unapologetically. Your guidance has been a lighthouse in the sometimes turbulent sea of self-expression.

And to my wonderful parents and sibling, whose unwavering belief in me has been a foundation for everything I choose to pursue. Your support has given me the wings to chase my dreams, and for that, I dedicate these words to you with all my heart.

Preface

Petals of the Unsaid is a collection inspired by the quiet intervals between our words—moments when emotions linger, unspoken yet profoundly felt. These poems are an expression of the innermost thoughts and feelings we often times harbor, the subtle murmurs of life and love, and hidden facets of ourselves.

I address the intricacies of moods, mental health, and the tiny shifts within our inner worlds in these verses, in addition to the beauty of relationships and the journey of love.

Each of these poems represents one of my many experiences, but more so, some of them invite you to contemplate upon yours. To me, life is a constant stream of unvoiced monologues and dialogues within one person, to other people, and to the outside world. And these undercurrents are where the core truths lie.

I emphasize that this is not merely a collection of poems – it is an excursion to the emptiness within us, the emptiness that consumes us. It's about the beauty of being vulnerable, the beauty of the voice, and the need to build a house where one can reside naked of flesh.

I hope these words are meaningful to you and help you accept the concept of how certain aspects are better left unsaid. They should reinforce the idea that there are pieces of the truth in each of us that are just waiting to bloom.

You are Just a Child!

You are just a child, oh dear child!
Life happened so swiftly for you.
The weight on your shoulders, the world threw,
And you were just a child!
An infant, eyes filled with innocence;
A toddler, with a heart that sought out love,
A child filled with only glimpses of joy,
You were just a child, dear child.
Never really understood the dynamics -
of this cruel world that swept you,
Your neck underwater, you were so lost,
You were just a child, oh child!
After all the cold years of childhood,
The moon was your only Robinhood,
Today you're all grown up, still seeking love,
You are still that little child, oh child!
You deserve all the world's happiness & love,
For you too are special in the universe's eye.
Be kind and compassionate, as always,
To love your inner child, oh dear child!

Am I Enough?

I often tend to ask myself,
Am I enough? Is all of this worth it?
What is the point of life, really?
Who am I even? What is my purpose?
Follows the self-doubts-filled masquerade.
Proceeded by tears of overwhelming confusion—
My gut says, "*I'm here to change the world*",
My heart and head disagree in doubt.
I can move people and perhaps mountains,
How do I get there to make all the difference?
Will I be stuck in this societal rut forever?
Will I ever have the 'will' to live free?
I know I often feel the weight of the world,
Getting heavier by the minute on my shoulders,
I take deep breaths to clear my mind,
And listen to my gut that says, "*I can be and I'm enough*".

Little Things

Them little things are bliss!
They can just make or break.
Them little things move mountains,
They can wreck worlds away!
It's the little things that make hearts melt,
Or cause the worst of heartbreaks.
You know, it is never the big things,
That give true feelings of fun or pain!
Little things, oh little things!
'Tis just a gesture or woven words -
Can make the best of memories,
That even Alzheimer's can defeat.
Little things, the very little things!
Are what make us human beings.
It's always the little things that make -
Us who we are today!

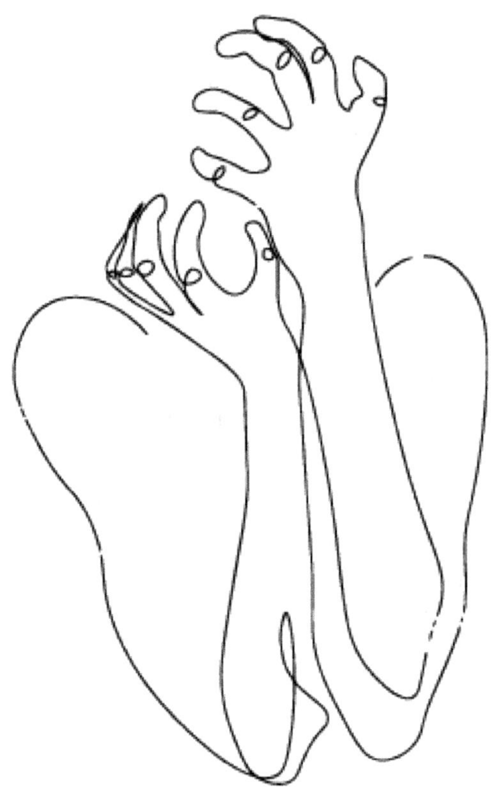

I'm So Tired

I'm so tired, I'm so dead!
After the spit-fire of words exchanged.
I wear my heart on my sleeve,
I am authentic, not so naive!
I can tolerate, I can endure,
The pain I've swallowed knows no cure,
I have a lot of love to give,
Don't push me too hard, for I will leave!
I love myself more than I did yesterday,
Self-respect and self-love are my everything,
I wouldn't let anyone take me for a ride,
Done with the people-pleasing, hell, I ride the
tide!
I do fear losing him in this tug-of-war,
He fades away a little, moving afar.
The man I love, I miss him so much,
Heavier is the price to win him back!

Game of Life

Believe in yourself, till the stars you will go,
Until you do not attempt, you'll never know.
Troubles sized in mountains and sorrows piled in
heaps,
Never give up anyway, these are but your deeds.
What others think of you is none of your business,
Ruminating on needless issues, life becomes a
mess!
Be yourself, try your best—keep these words in
mind;
If so, you'll never feel betrayed and you'll never
have to wind!
The journey has some potholes, stay aware and
awake,
How you take it all - is how you're going to make.
Make life worth living, it's all about how you play
Think wise, be nice, don't end up on the slippery
slope.
Life is a simple game, played by everyone around,
The only game that you'll always play, from the
time you're born.
Live every moment of life, like it is your absolute
last,
'Cause every day's a party, just go have a blast!

Life is Hard

Oh yes, it happens to me all the time!
Having questions or confusion, ain't a crime.
Yes! Life can be hard and full of hurdles,
Like the saying, "It ain't a bed full of roses".
Obstacles, heartaches, dead-ends, depression,
Many such blockages are but lessons!
While you're amidst a sticky situation,
Face it! Embrace it! Don't yield! Don't run!
I never claim life to be easy, for it's not -
But the remedy is to love yourself the most,
It gives you the fire to face the worst,
You now know what to do, go be your best!
Be your best in the world of 'loving you',
Everything from that moment will seem anew.
Love yourself, love others, do good and stay
humble,
The more you do so, the less you're likely to
stumble!

Am I a Butterfly?

Am I a butterfly?
Oh, can I be one? Though—
I don't enjoy change!
I'm just a caterpillar in a cage.
I like my cage,
The dark and cozy corners,
I believe in the known devil
That's better than an unknown angel.
When I look back,
At the 30 years of my life,
Familiarity and comfort,
Was where I thrived, 'twas my stride.
The fear of the unknown seemed too daunting!
But one fine day, I chose to step out of this
haunting,
Ever since, I've been free, authentic, and a pretty
wild butterfly,
Accepting change, though it's hard, is how I can
be better!

A Little Girl

I am just a little girl,
Behind those very tall walls.
I portray a strong and independent swirl,
Yet deep down, I'm just a little girl.
During my times of achievement,
And all those phases of depression,
I always stood back up,
I was still just a little girl inside.
I'm just like fine wine,
I have gracefully aged with time,
I still would prefer my sweet lime,
As I still carry that little girl's chime.
I look up to the world with a spark in my eyes,
I'm vulnerable with my arms open wide.
I give so much love, and not I seek,
I am just a little girl, with hope-filled dreams!

Back to the Shore

What does loneliness even feel like?
Amidst big crowds, your heart starts to strike;
Strike and outcry, failing to feel the love around,
Turning cold and numb, worse than barren
ground!
Why is life often gifted with jolts like these?
Never a smooth medley like 'wine and cheese'.
At times neither moments nor memories do
please,
It is such a rugged journey; as messy as grease!
Why does everything shatter, all at once?
Recovering is uncertain, takes weeks or months.
It takes beyond everything to repair what's
broken-
Deep scars and wounds leave the soul forsaken!
I was known to be the 'happy-go-lucky-girl',
With a smile that shone brighter than pearl!
Lost in the ocean of darkness, where do I explore?
How do I get my old self back to the shore?

True Love

What really is love? A mystery? A puzzle?
It's full of life and overdosed with dazzle!
It's mistaken for lust and sometimes, luxury,
Fighting for true love is but sheer bravery!
Life seems meaningless without this only element,
Enriched and engraved in every little fragment—
Every little fragment which completes the only
maze;
The maze called true love that can make any soul
daze!
Love is the only invention of the almighty,
Some call it dangerous while some call it Godly.
What really is true love? Is it for real?
It is as real as life is and anything can be!
'Tis a connection that speaks without
communication.
A devotion truly like that of a patriot to the
nation.
A crazy feeling that makes one alive and equally
dead;
True love is simply divine; neither can it be
depicted nor said!!!

Crazy Stupid Love

Life was getting hard, with lifeless days,
Figuring out 'one day at a time', in about 100 ways,
They say, 'At the end of the tunnel, a bright light
awaits!'
When I started walking towards it, 'twas love's
holy grail!
Them voices in my head, *"You sure of what's going
on?"*
"Is this even normal or is this the age of Ultron?!"
Every breath, every moment seemed so fast-paced,
I had to hold my horses, to hypostatize!
Was it a cosmic connection? Do 'soulmates' really
exist?
The fire signs in the Zodiac world were drinking
Zeus's antiquities.
Our union would leave the town painted red with
wildfire,
We would be twin flames, our dance could burn a
thousand shires.
It was but a miracle and pure magic did exist,
Crazy stupid love, like racing through heavy mist!
You have stolen my heart but, have I stolen yours?
'Tis the mystery - I'm yet to unveil.

The Queen of Hills

Our car drives and long nights,
Shiny Betty, well in her prime,
She roared like a rockstar, every time—
He hit the gas to the nine!
The hilly curves, the hairpin bends,
The drops of rain on the misty terrain,
A memorable drive, indeed it was;
Happy and high, we reached at last!
The Queen of Hills, oh so magnificent!
Her beauty was nothing short of decadent.
The air smelt heavenly, oh so pure,
Her offerings, oh so sweet! so far, yet so near.
The towns in the valley shone like diamonds,
Oh nature! you spoke so loud in silence!
An experience worth a hundred lifetimes -
She humbled us all, with her existence.

Oh my Love, Oh my Dear

Oh my eyes, Oh my eyes
They constantly look for you!
Oh my ears, Oh my ears,
They long to hear your voice.
Oh my nose, Oh my nose,
They yearn for the smell of your skin!
Oh my lips, Oh my lips,
They eagerly await your soft, love-filled kiss.
Oh my skin, Oh my skin,
They search for your warmth and touch!
Oh my hands, Oh my hands,
They miss wrapping you in them.
Oh my mind, Oh my heart,
They just so need you right now!
Oh my love, Oh my everything,
Even a wall away seems like you're planets apart.

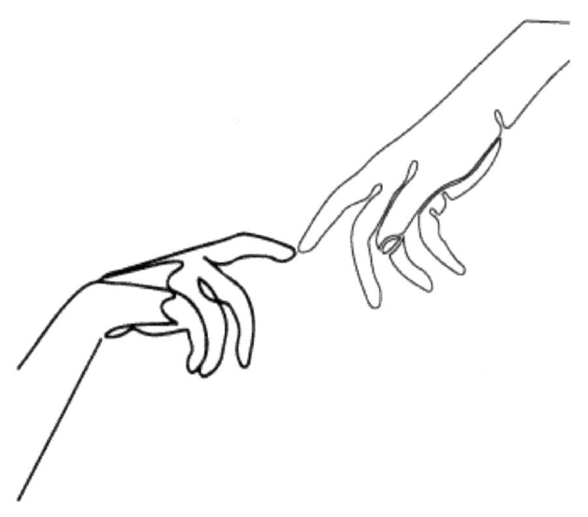

Essence of My Being

My Darling, Oh Darling,
I love the way you smile!
On a gloomy, cloudy day,
Your smile can brighten the sky!
My Darling, Oh Darling,
Do you know? You are my world
For without you in my life,
There is but just a void!
My Darling, Oh Darling,
I love the person you are,
My partner, best friend and confidant,
Nurturing my fragile heart!
My Darling, Oh Darling,
Don't you see what you mean to me?
My life itself, and so much more;
You are the essence of my being!

Sins of Her Past

All she did was propose to him!
For she was a happy and naive girl,
Who was taught that the world was bright,
So protected from the horror of blues!
She was but a flower that had blossomed in time,
In the sunniest and most beautiful shades!
Little did she know what she had stepped into,
For her life would soon be a chaotic mess!
Her vibrant soul, full of positivity and naïveté,
Led her down a dangerous path,
She always knew she could trust those she loved,
Soon, the world wronged her and murdered her
trust!
Every time she thought, things would get better,
'Twas two steps forward and ten steps back.
She was taught that her life was 'all about giving',
But all she ever got back were the sins of her past!

Will you marry me?

'Love' was the word that stood out best in my
dictionary,
For my persona, it was something contrary!
I had no time to think of anyone else,
What a surprise! I found myself in a beautiful
mess.
Life never seemed so perfect and in place,
We were meant to be like Satin and Lace.
It's true like the saying, 'Falling in love is an
accident'
In my aura, you were the mesmerizing scent.
'Live your life to the fullest' was what I believed
in,
'It just got better' I told myself, with a grin,
As days passed by, I lost myself to you,
Three years done, yet it still feels afresh and new!
To dream of us living life together forever,
Wow! We'd be like Volcanoes and tremors!
Your words, 'Will you marry me?' still linger in my
ears,
It's a 'Yes' baby! I always want you near!

You Came Like a Dream

I can be brave, I can be strong,
When it comes to you, I'm proven wrong!
The wave of insecurity is already washing away,
The shores of my life from sunny to grey!
The moment you disclose the decision you've
made,
It may be a gift or perhaps a sharp blade.
Everything seemed so bright though uncertain,
Now that I reside on the dark side of the
mountain.
I've gone too numb to even feel the breeze gushing
over me,
In your love, I have become a terrible spree!
You're the spark that I see in the crowd,
You already seem to blur out, your absence is
loud!
You came like a dream—a bright flash of
happiness,
Now all that I see is that I've landed up in a mess!
I'm a mess without you and I could go blind,
'Cause with you starts my day, with you it'll wind!

My Ride or Die!

We are two peas in a pod!
And time has proven that -
Time and time again,
We are each other's 'Forever and always'.
The hottie on the Stunner,
Who picked me up for a ride,
Asking me for a roll-to-go,
I stood watching him hog!
When I look back today,
To our past; full of adventures,
I gleam with gratitude and joy,
For you wanted to be mine!
The little arguments that we had,
Broke my heart, and I picked up the pieces,
Gluing the million pieces back again,
For you'll always be my ride or die!

Bread and Butter

I miss you more than words can convey,
I love you unconditionally, come what may,
With you, I cannot wait to grow old and grey,
Not a moment passes without your thoughts, oh
hey!
Whatever the season be—summer or spring,
Without you around, all I feel are jitters,
Me and you together - it can't get any better,
We are made for each other like bread and butter.
We might argue, or make love,
We communicate, celebrate, and make it right.
Love keeps us going for it was at first sight,
In my darkness, you are the only light.
Our blend is as perfect as tequila and lime,
Me and you—two bodies, one soul, just fine.
It sure proves, our marriage was made in heaven,
It's because of your love I'm always on cloud nine.

I'm Yours

I'm so full of your love in me,
This is how I always wanted it to be,
More than myself, I think of you,
It's so overwhelming, it's so new.
The moment I saw you on your knees
You looked like a prince, believe me, please!
Your words, your looks, your wonderful smile,
Let me be mesmerized in your world for a while!
It's like I lived my whole life with you,
To have you with me, I'm lucky among the few.
The togetherness and the feeling of being secure,
Your absence, your silence I just can't endure!
I'm so used to you, and only you I can see,
Blindfolded in your charm, I'd love to be!
I'm blessed to be 'the one', to be all yours!
I promise to be your only one and the future is all
ours!

All that Starts Well Ends Well

As I sit at my desk sipping hot coffee,
Dreaming if I'd ink my 'love story'
Missing the good times spent with him for hours,
I am already drenched in solitary showers.
Life was at its best speed when we weren't so busy,
Lost in planning our future, I was so fussy!
Cuddling and holding hands, we found our
'nirvana'
Responsibilities and routines are now the new
phenomena.
Whenever I am idle, I long to be with him -
Keeping myself busy with yoga or gym,
However hard I try, I cannot get over his
thoughts!
His absence puts me on edge, my heart tangled in
knots.
All that I do is shed tears profusely,
With his void in my world, I've become so timid.
My heart and soul feel like an empty shell,
I feel hopeful reminding myself, 'All that starts
well ends well'!